MOTHERLY LOVE

CELEBRATING THE MOTHER-BABY BOND AT THE WORLD'S ZOOS AND AQUARIUMS

Andrew Bleiman and Chris Eastland

SIMON & SCHUSTER PAPERBACKS

New York London Toronto Sydney New Delhi

Simon & Schuster Paperbacks
An Imprint of Simon & Schuster, Inc.
1230 Avenue of the Americas
New York, NY 10020

First Simon & Schuster trade paperback edition October 2022

SIMON & SCHUSTER PAPERBACKS and colophon are registered trademarks of Simon & Schuster, Inc.

For information about special discounts for bulk purchases, please contact Simon & Schuster Special
Sales at 1-866-506-1949 or business@simonandschuster.com.

The Simon & Schuster Speakers Bureau can bring authors to your live event. For more information, or
to book an event, contact the Simon & Schuster Speakers Bureau at 1-866-248-3049
or visit our website at www.simonspeakers.com.

Interior design by Chris Eastland
Cover design by Chris Eastland

Manufactured in the United States of America

10 9 8 7 6 5 4 3 2 1

The Library of Congress has cataloged the hardcover edition as follows:

Bleiman, Andrew.
   ZooBorns motherly love : celebrating the mother-baby bond at the world's zoos and aquariums /
Andrew Bleiman and Chris Eastland.
      pages cm
   ISBN 978-1-4767-9196-8 (hardcover)—ISBN 978-1-4767-9197-5 (ebook) 1. Zoo animals—Infancy—
Pictorial works. 2. Parental behavior in animals—Pictorial works. I. Eastland, Chris. II. Title. III. Title:
Zoo borns motherly love.
   QL77.5.B5394 2015
   591.3'92073--dc23
                                                                          2014036557

ISBN 978-1-4767-9196-8
ISBN 978-1-6680-1342-7 (pbk)
ISBN 978-1-4767-9197-5 (ebook)

MOTHERLY LOVE

CELEBRATING THE MOTHER-BABY BOND AT THE WORLD'S ZOOS AND AQUARIUMS

Andrew Bleiman and Chris Eastland

Introduction

"Mother knows best" rings true throughout much of the animal kingdom. That's why modern zoos and aquariums look to their animal moms to raise their babies whenever possible.

For many species, newborns rely on mom for nourishment, be it milk or worms, as well as comfort and protection. As ZooBorns grow, they look to mom to teach essential survival skills like hunting, grooming, and socializing.

While mom takes the lead, specialized veterinarians, biologists, and keepers at Association of Zoos and Aquariums accredited facilities often provide supplementary care. Just like with a human baby, preventative medical assessments and regular observation facilitate early detection and treatment during the first few critical days, weeks, and months.

The more you know about animals and the mother-baby bond, the more you, too, can protect them. So, turn the page and meet the animal moms and their precious ZooBorns. Then, visit your local accredited zoo or aquarium to learn more!

—Paul Boyle, PhD
Senior Vice President for Conservation R+D and Policy
Association of Zoos and Aquariums

**ASSOCIATION
OF ZOOS &
AQUARIUMS**

*A portion of all proceeds from ZooBorns book sales goes directly to
the AZA's Conservation Endowment Fund*

The IUCN Red List of Threatened Species is the world's most comprehensive inventory of the global conservation status of biological species. In this book we highlight species in the following categories:

Critically endangered **CR** – Extremely high risk of extinction in the wild

Endangered **EN** – High risk of extinction in the wild

Vulnerable **VU** – High risk of endangerment in the wild

Near threatened **NT** – Likely to become endangered in the near future

Least concern **LC** – Lowest risk. Does not qualify for a more at risk category. Widespread and abundant taxa are included in this category

Data deficient **DD** – Not enough data to make an assessment of its risk of extinction

Northern Sea Otter VU

Mother sea otters are experts at keeping their pups afloat on the waves! Immediately after birth, they begin a multi-hour grooming session, licking and fluffing their babies' fur until it is puffed-up full of air. The little baby is so buoyant it couldn't sink even if it wanted to! When mom leaves to forage, she will often wrap her baby in kelp to keep it from floating away.

Sekiu was born to ten-year-old mom Aniak at the Seattle Aquarium. In the wild, mother otters separate their pups from larger males. Seattle Aquarium gave Aniak and Sekiu private space to bond for the first seven months.

C.J. Casson / Seattle Aquarium

11

Pygmy Hippopotamus EN
Tampa's Lowry Park Zoo, Florida

Meet Zola, a healthy pygmy hippo calf born to second-time Lowry Park Zoo mom, Zsa Zsa. "Regular" adult hippopotamuses can weigh 18,000 lbs (8,150 kg) or more but little Zola weighed only 10 lbs (4.5kg) at birth.

15

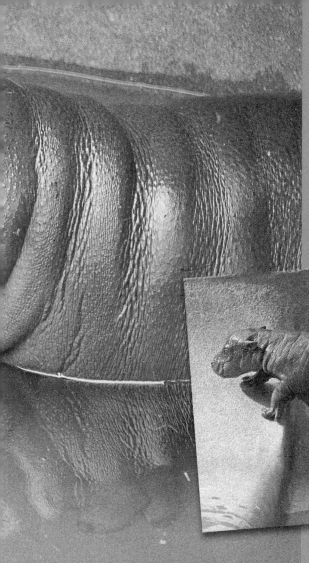

Before heading out to forage, mother pygmy hippos hide their calves partially submerged in the swamp. When they return, they croak, grunt, and honk to call their babies to nurse.

Shy and elusive, pygmy hippos are famously difficult to study in their densely forested native habitat. Consequently, almost everything known about their parenting comes from observing them at zoos.

Polar Bear  VU
Zoo Vienna, Austria

In the late fall, pregnant mother polar bears build cozy dens in snowdrifts. Two months later they give birth, typically to two cubs. The family will not emerge until spring, which means mama bear goes without eating for four to eight months!

Polar bear cubs are totally dependent on mom for survival for almost two years. Her hunting skills will determine whether the whole family is well fed.

This cub, named Arktos, is one of two healthy baby boys born at Zoo Vienna to mother Olinka. Mother bears nuzzle muzzles with their cubs to demonstrate affection and strengthen bonds.

© Shedd Aquarium / Brenna Hernandez

22

Beluga Whale NT
Shedd Aquarium, Chicago, Illinois

Baby belugas nurse from mom for a full year before their teeth come in and they start nibbling on shrimp and squid. During this time, other female belugas will often pitch in to help, even providing milk. Studying whales underwater in the Arctic is challenging (cold!), so much of what we know about beluga whale parenting comes from aquariums.

A happy, healthy tyke at 450 lbs (204 kg) at the time of these photos, it's hard to believe Nunavik almost did not survive his first day in the water. Born head-first instead of tail-first, the calf was saved by hands-on care during the delivery by Shedd's marine mammal team. Today Nunavik loves nothing more than to mimic the antics of his mom, Puiji, and enrichment time, which includes interacting with marine mammal experts, playing with toys, and solving puzzles with Shedd aquarists.

Somali Wild Ass CR

Ramat Gan Zoological Society, Israel
Saint Louis Zoo, Missouri, United States
Woburn Safari Park, UK

Believed to be the ancestor of the domestic donkey, today the Somali wild ass is among the world's rarest mammals. While the exact size of the wild, critically endangered population is unknown, it's estimated to be only a few hundred.

These foals were born at three different zoos: Saint Louis Zoo in the United States; Woburn Safari Park in England; and the Ramat Gan Zoological Center in Tel Aviv, Israel. Zoos often coordinate breeding efforts to ensure a diverse gene pool. Some day this critical zoo population of about two hundred animals might prove instrumental in repopulating the species in the wild.

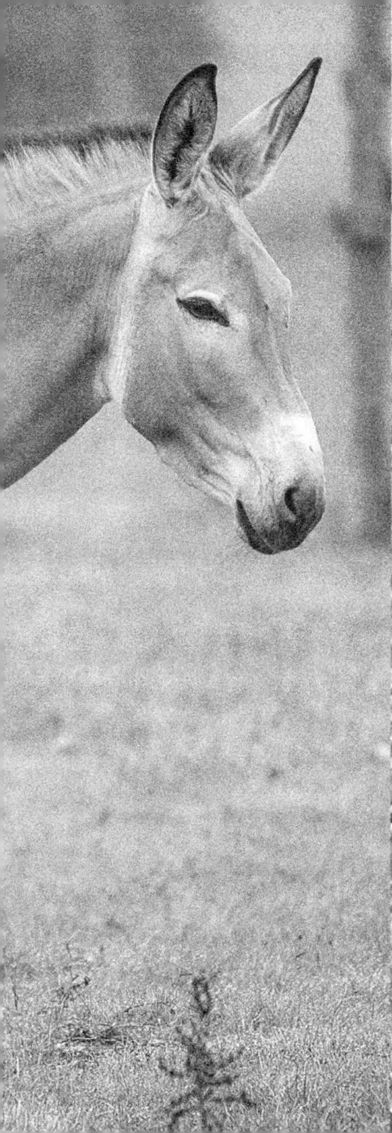

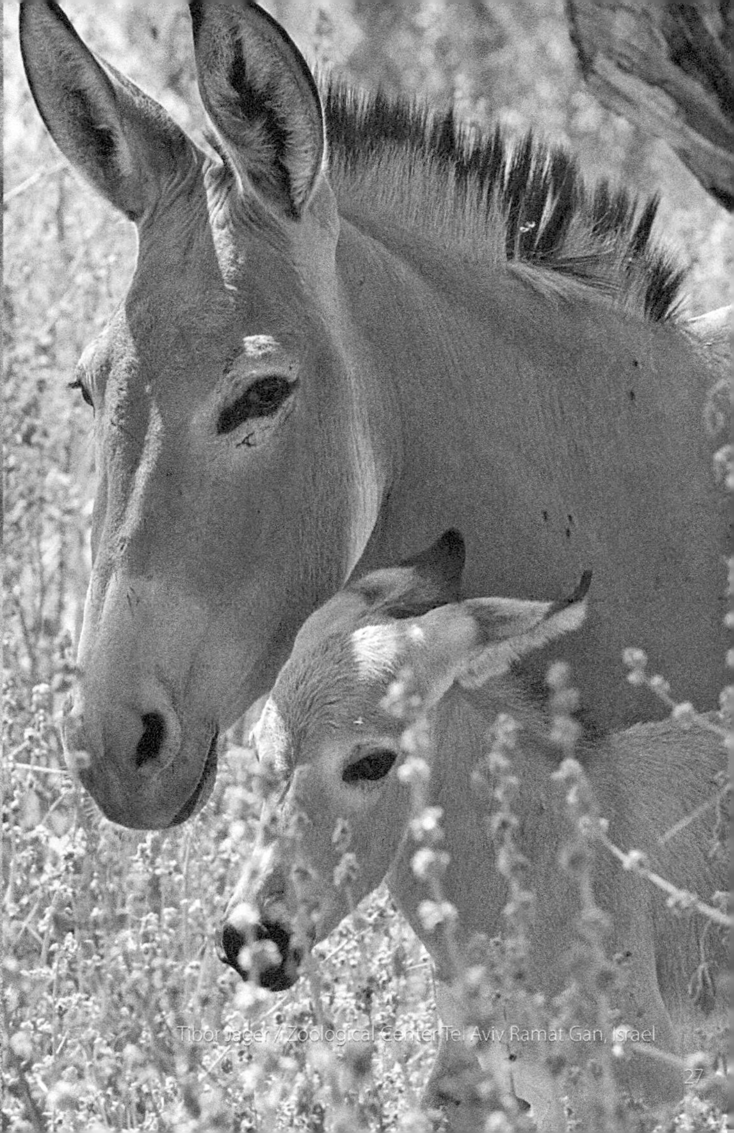

Tibor Jager / Zoological Center Tel Aviv Ramat Gan, Israel

Cheetah VU
Chester Zoo, UK

At two months old, Chester Zoo's cheetah cubs were "very, very playful and a real handful for mum, KT." Luckily this was the second litter for KT and she proved to be an excellent parent to these rambunctious cubs. Scientists estimate only about 250 northern cheetahs remain in the wild.

Chester Zoo

Patagonian Mara LC
Cotswold Wildlife Park & Gardens, UK

Shy and speedy, these Patagonian mara pups were hard to photograph! Unlike their close relatives, rabbits and guinea pigs, Patagonian mara mate for life. Males spend most of their day vigilantly guarding their mate from predators. As their name suggest, this species is native only to the dry deserts, steppes, and mountains of Patagonia.

Theo Kruse / Burgers' Zoo

Western Lowland Gorilla ⒸⓇ

Royal Burgers' Zoo, Netherlands

While keepers knew gorilla N'Gayla was pregnant, they got a big surprise when they discovered she had given birth to twins, which are much rarer for gorillas than humans. Much like human babies, baby gorillas are helpless and require round-the-clock feeding. Fortunately N'Gayla was an experienced mother totally up to the challenge!

Baby gorillas ride on mom's back up to age two or three, but rely on mom for food, comfort, and protection for another year or two after that.

In the wild Western lowland, gorillas are threatened by habitat destruction, diseases like Ebola, and hunting. Organizations like the Wildlife Conservation Society's Bronx Zoo have pioneered innovative efforts to save this species, like working with local African communities to develop alternatives to poaching.

Mandarin Duck LC

Mandarin duck pairs house hunt together, looking for the perfect tree hollow close to the water's edge. Mom then covers the bottom of the nest with down and lays up to twelve eggs. Amazingly all the eggs hatch within hours of each other, twenty eight to thirty days later.

Even though mom can build her nest up to thirty feet off the ground, she encourages her whole brood to leap out of the roost within hours of hatching and the ducklings land unhurt on the ground. Mom then leads her duckling parade to the nearest body of water to start snacking.

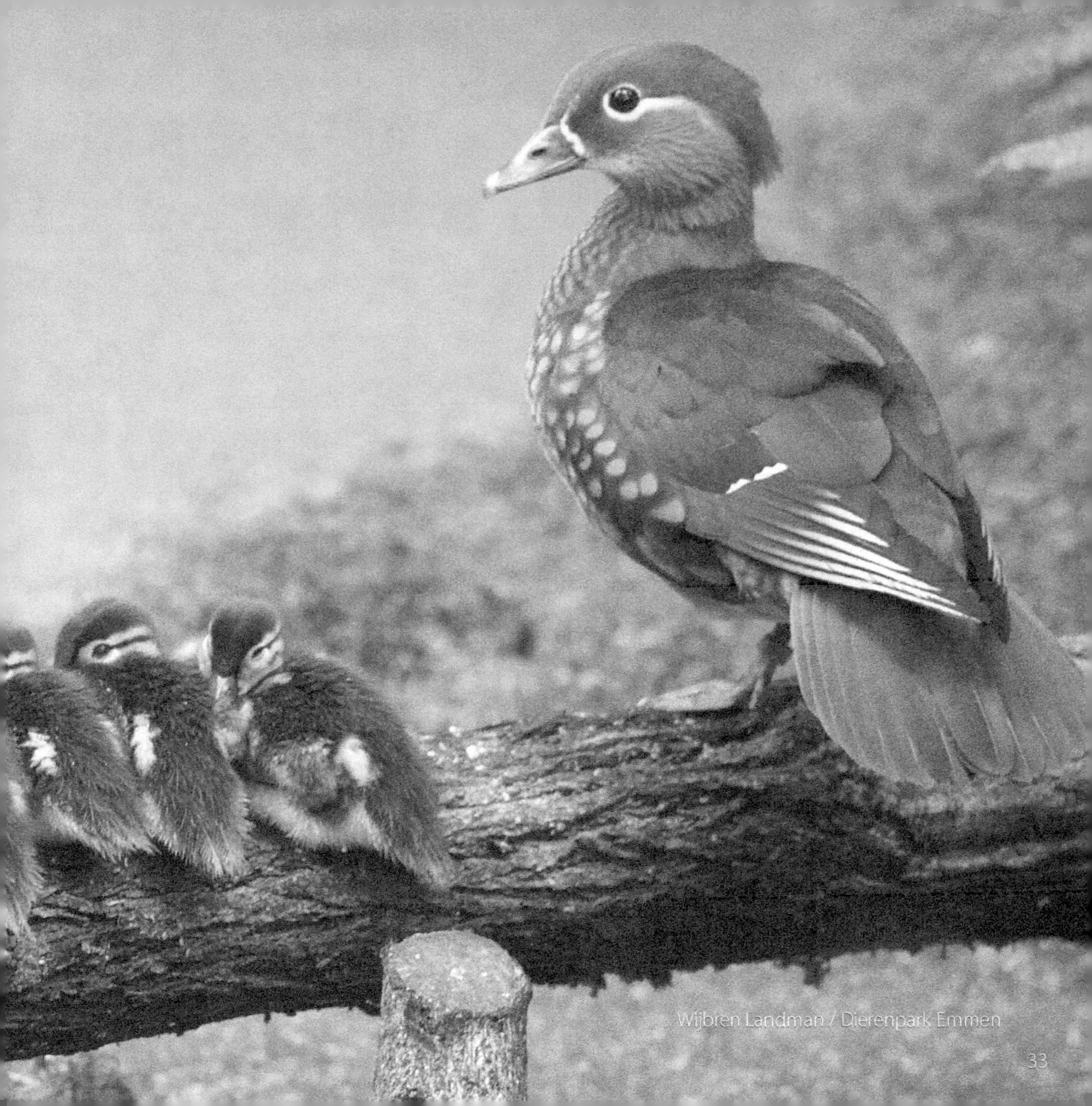
Wijbren Landman / Dierenpark Emmen

European Bison

VU

Port Lympne Wild Animal Park, UK

Hunted to extinction in the wild in the first half of the 20th Century, the European bison has staged a comeback thanks to breeding programs like the one at Port Lympne Wild Animal Park. Many of the bison born here are released into the Carpathian Mountains in Romania as part of a coordinated reintroduction effort. This young female will join that growing population once she matures and has calves of her own.

Black-breasted Leaf Turtle

Fort Wayne Children's Zoo, Indiana

Responsible parenting for black-breasted leaf turtles means laying eggs in a secluded place and carefully covering the clutch to ensure they are out of sight (and smell!) of predators. These eggs were carefully collected by keepers at Fort Wayne Children's Zoo and kept safe and toasty at 78 degrees. In the wild, most turtle moms will never meet their hatchlings, but these two shared a rare reptilian-Kodak-moment.

Fort Wayne Children's Zoo

Quokka
Perth Zoo, Australia

Resembling a small, stocky kangaroo, the quokka is a highly social Australian marsupial with little to no fear of humans. Quokka moms give birth to a single joey. The pink, helpless baby crawls into mom's pouch and spends its first six months safely tucked away.

Most wild quokkas live on Rottnest Island, so named because early Dutch explorers mistook these strange animals for big rats. Who could make that mistake!?

African Painted Dog

Perth Zoo, Australia

After eight weeks in the den, African painted dog mother, Mara, ventured outside for the first time with her healthy litter of seven at Perth Zoo. Females of this species have their work cut out for them, sometimes giving birth to as many as nineteen puppies!

Luckily for mom, African painted dogs are highly social. The full pack will share the responsibility of raising the young, including feeding them. Unusual among canines, adult male painted dogs will often stay behind to guard the pups while the rest of the pack hunts.

Canada Lynx LC
Minnesota Zoo, Apple Valley, Minnesota

Minnesota Zoo staff ensured peace and quiet for this first time Canada lynx mom by closing the exhibit to the public and providing her with a private behind-the-scenes nest box. This approach allowed mom to focus on bonding with her kittens, all four of which appear happy and healthy.

Born blind and helpless, Canada lynx kittens open their beautiful, blue eyes after about two weeks. Mom weans her young at about two months and brings them live prey to hone their hunting skills!

Tomáš Adamec / Zoo Praha

Mishmi Takin EN

Zoo Praha, Czech Republic

This rare goat-antelope roams the remote, foggy mountains spanning China, India, Bhutan, and Myanmar. Within three days of birth, takin calves can follow their mothers through the rugged, steep, and rocky terrain they call home.

Endangered in the wild due to poaching, Mishmi Takin have thrived in breeding programs like the one at Prague Zoo, which has welcomed four calves since 2001.

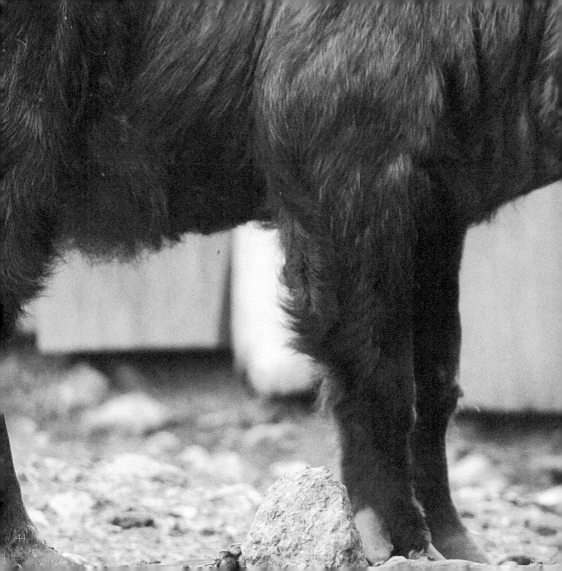

Fennec Fox LC
Drusillas Park, UK

Meet Mali, dubbed Fantastic Mrs. Fox by the Drusillas Park keepers for successfully raising seven cubs since her arrival in 2009, as part of the European Association of Zoos and Aquaria breeding program. Shy and skittish, Fennec foxes often don't feel comfortable enough in a zoo environment to breed, so Mali's success represents the Zoo's dedication to providing comfortable conditions.

Fennec foxes mate for life. The male aggressively protects the female and feeds her throughout the pregnancy, standing guard until he can greet his cubs.

Giant Panda (EN)
San Diego Zoo, California

Little Xiao Liwu was mother panda Bai Yun's sixth cub since arriving at the San Diego Zoo in 2006; a record for panda moms outside of China! Mom began playfully wrestling with her cub at just three months, teaching valuable survival skills while strengthening their bond.

While the giant panda population was steady before human habitat destruction, biologically speaking it seems like the species wasn't exactly set up for reproductive success. . . . Female pandas are fertile for just two to three days in a given year. What's more, their newborns are proportionately the smallest of any mammal other than marsupials and mono-tremes (i.e. platypuses). While giant pandas can weigh up to 350 lbs (160 kg), their babies weigh just three to five ounces (85–140 g); about the size of a small russet potato!

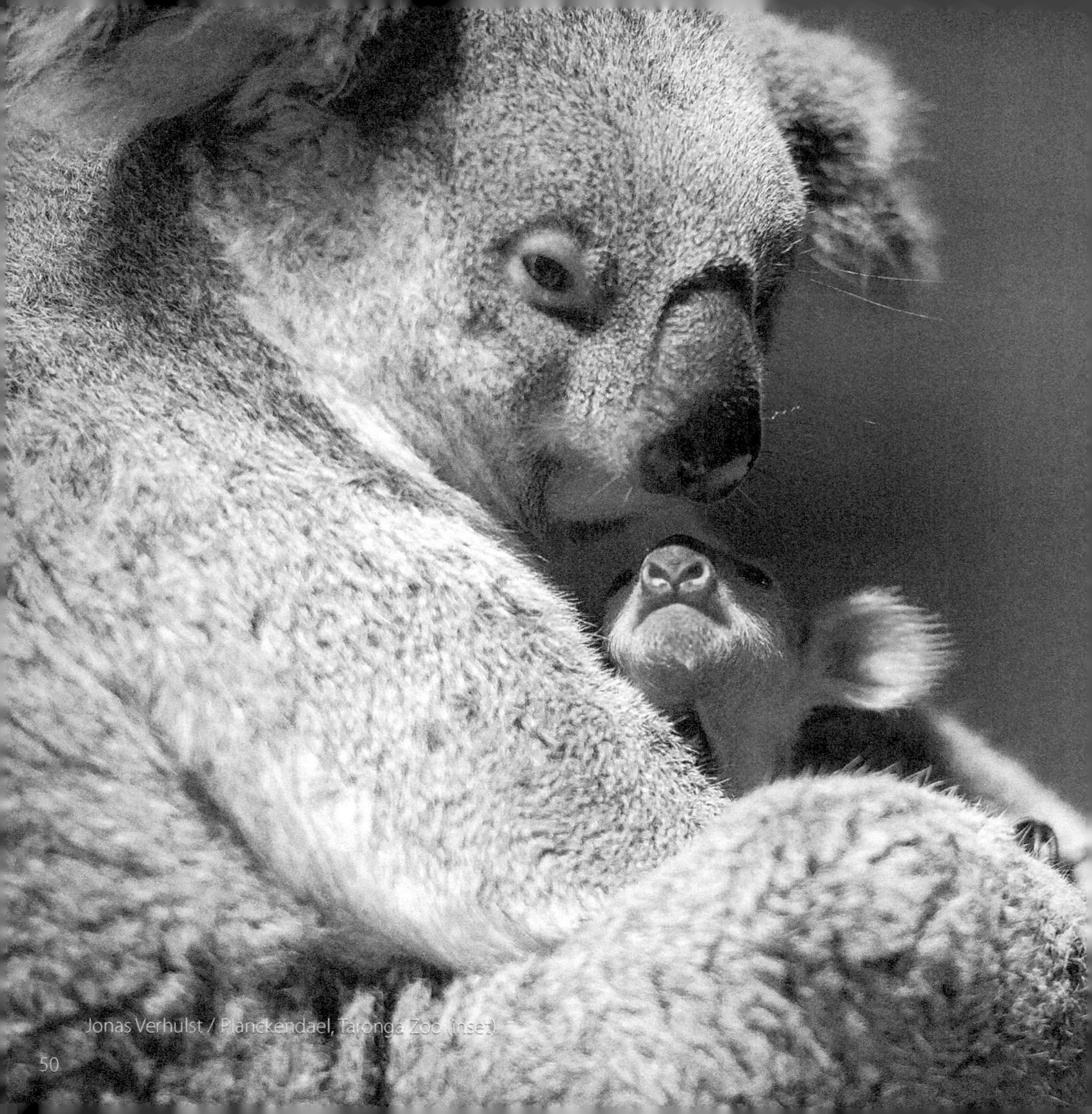
Jonas Verhulst / Planckendael, Taronga Zoo (inset)

Koala LC

Planckendael, Belgium
Taronga Zoo, Australia

Koala joeys first poke their head out from mom's pouch around six months of age; at around nine months, they graduate to riding on mom's back. Subsisting exclusively on nutrient-poor eucalyptus means koala milk is also low in nutrition, so mother koalas compensate by nursing their joeys for a full year.

Peter Bolliger / Zoo Zürich

Tibetan Wolf LC

Zoo Zurich, Switzerland

Mother wolves get a lot of help raising their young; the whole pack pitches in. Younger and related females will often be designated "babysitters," responsible for watching the pups while mom is hunting. If a pack mother goes missing, other females will often adopt her pups and raise them.

Believed to be the ancestor of the domestic dog, Tibetan wolves are a subspecies of the wide-ranging gray wolf. Tibetan wolves occasionally take livestock, so they face their biggest threat from indigenous farmers and herders who don't tolerate their presence near their animals.

Big-eyed Tree Frog  EN
Staten Island Zoo, New York

In the wild, big-eyed tree frogs lay their eggs on the banks of streams. When the tadpoles hatch, they wiggle their way into the water. At Staten Island Zoo, mother tree frogs lay their eggs in moss and the tadpoles wiggle their way through false bottoms made of mesh into a bowl of water below after they hatch. The tadpoles have spectacularly long tails, possibly to help them move from land to the water.

After the tadpoles morph into frogs, they climb into trees along the edge of the stream. The juveniles' green color helps them blend in among the leaves for their first few months. Eventually, they will turn brown and settle into a life on the forest floor.

Harpy Eagle  NT
Zoo Miami, Florida

Zoo Miami staff were eager to check on their newest harpy eagle chick but mom would have none of it. "The mother gets very defensive, opens her wings and covers the chick right away. Then she starts squealing . . . wheeee wheeee wheee. And when a bird has talons the size of a grizzly bear's paw, you pay attention," explained Zoo Miami's spokesman.

Among the largest of all birds of prey, harpy eagles mate for life and raise one chick every two to three years. They build their nests in the highest branches of the kapok tree, one of South America's tallest trees, out of the reach of most predators. However if a would be egg-eater does find its way to the nest, they have to deal with mom's formidable talons, which are the largest of any eagle.

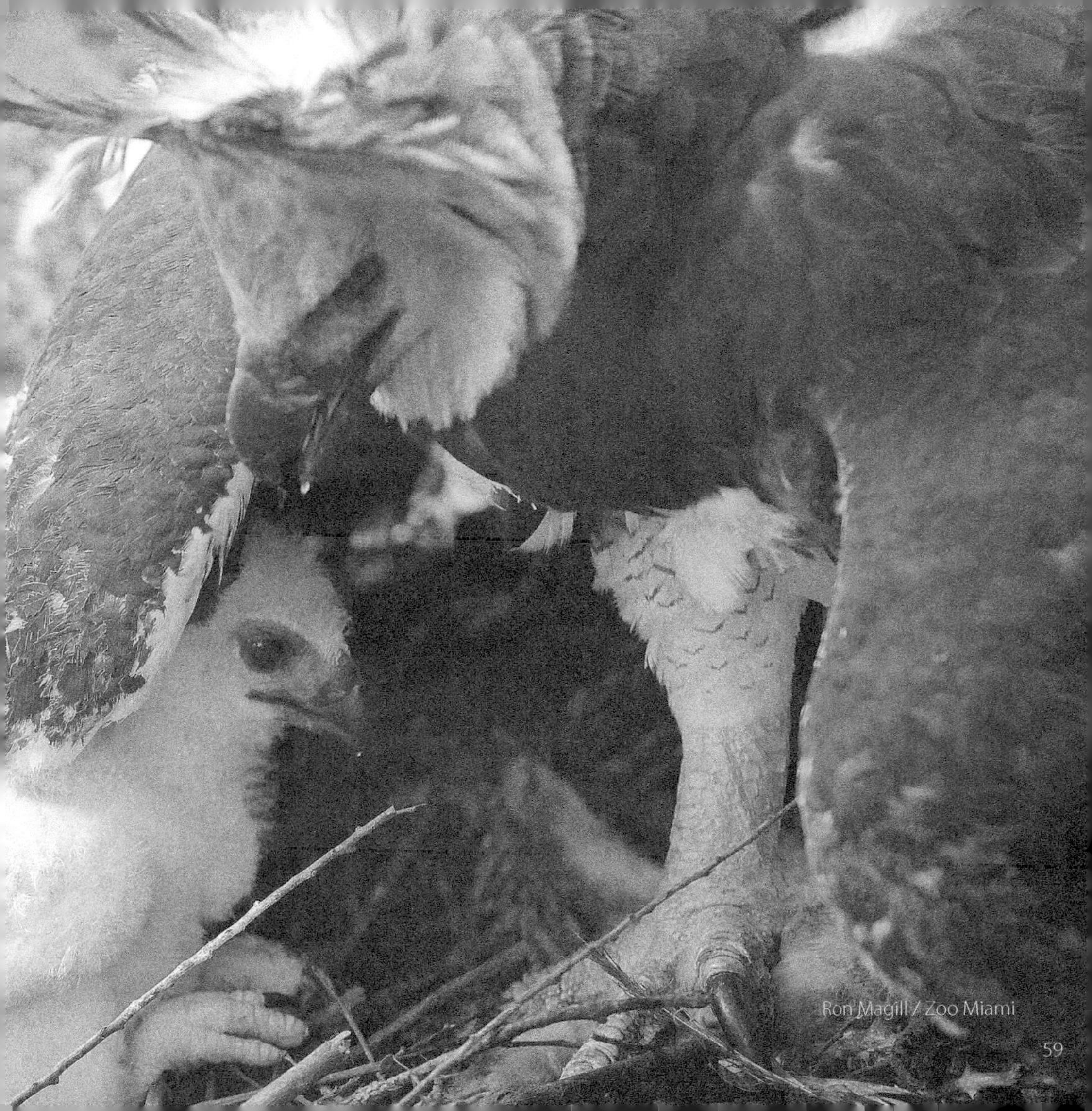

Ron Magill / Zoo Miami

Java Mousedeer DD

Zoo Zürich, Switzerland

Weighing less than 4 lbs (1.8 kg), the Java mousedeer is
among the world's smallest hoofed mammals. Their tiny
fawns weigh less than one pound at birth. Amazingly, female
mousedeer can become pregnant again just two and a half
hours after giving birth!

Corinne Invernizzi / Zoo Zürich, Peter Bolliger / Zoo Zürich (inset)

Dhole EN

Minnesota Zoo, Apple Valley, Minnesota

In 2012 Minnesota Zoo had a dhole baby-boom with
two moms giving birth within two days. Since dholes'
pack-mates share parenting duties, determining
whose baby was whose was challenging!

Common Gundi LC

Artis Royal Zoo, Netherlands

Baby gundis like this one keep warm by nuzzling up underneath the soft fur of their mothers' necks. Native to dry African deserts, gundi moms provide very little milk and babies are weaned at two months.

Arjan Haverkamp taken at Artis Royal Zoo

Southern Tamandua LC

Meet MJ, the little Southern Tamandua born to mom, DJ, and dad, EJ. Tamanduas, also known as lesser anteaters, give birth to a single baby each year. Young tamanduas spend most of their lives riding on mom's back, although mom may drop them off on a tree branch when she needs a little personal time to forage.

Anteaters have no teeth and rely on their specialized stomachs to mash up their mostly insect diet.

Steve Yensel / Staten Island Zoo

Przewalski's Horse CR

Zoo Praha, Czech Republic
Port Lympne Wild Animal Park, UK

Przewalski's horse is considered the only true wild horse species left in the world. It was officially extinct in the wild before innovative zoo breeding programs brought the species back from the brink. Today, fifty wild horses live in their native home of Mongolia thanks to breeding at zoos like Port Lympne and reintroduction efforts led by Zoo Praha.

Tomáš Adamec / Zoo Praha, Dave Rolfe / Port Lympne Wild Animal Park (inset)

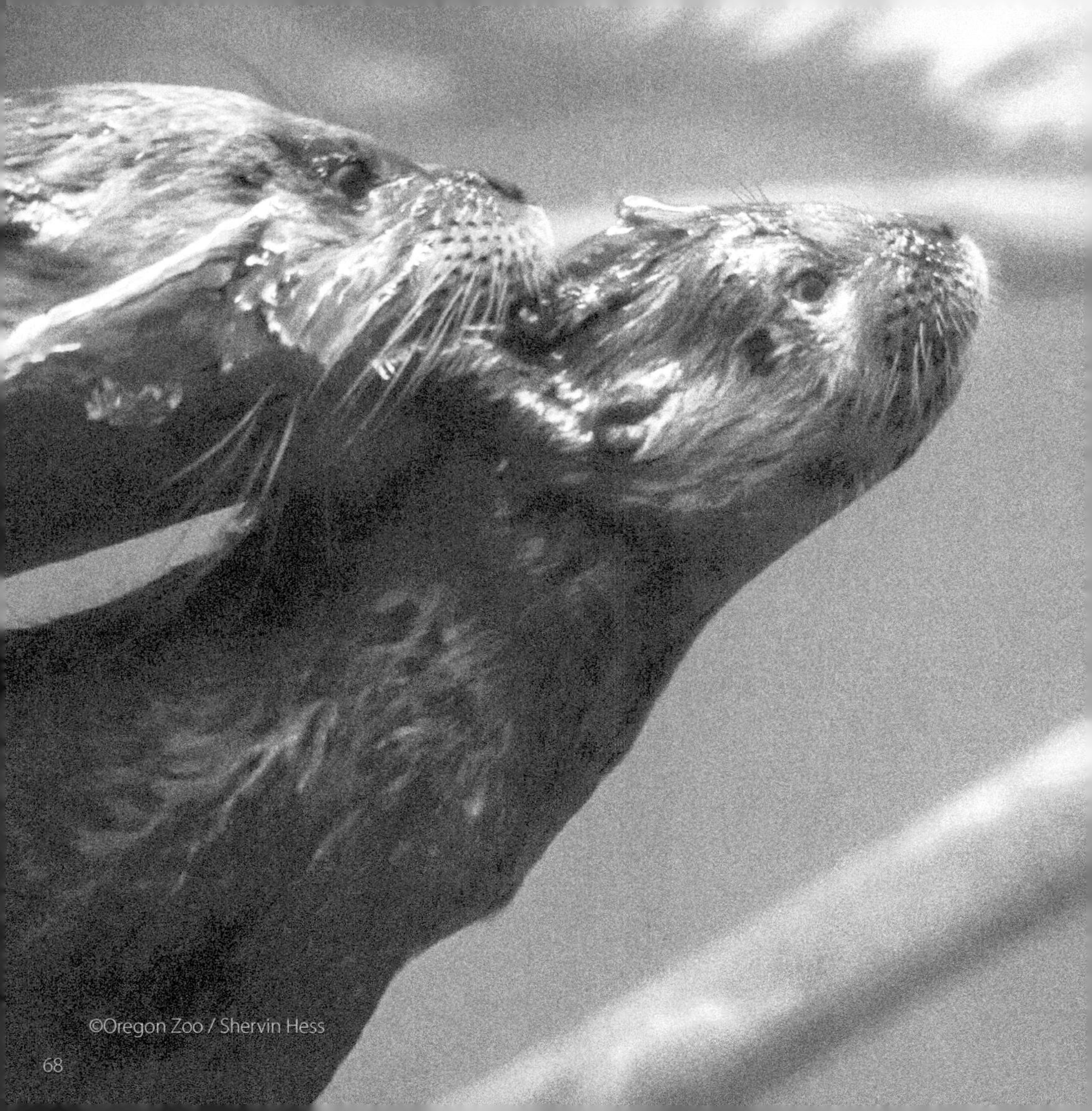

North American River Otter LC

Ziggy, a two-month-old North American river otter at the Oregon Zoo, learned to swim with the help of his mom, Tilly. "Otter pups are very dependent on their mother and they don't know how to swim right away," explained Senior Keeper Christie. "The mother actually has to teach them."

Tilly nudges her pup to the water's edge and then plunges in with a firm grip on the scruff of his neck, just as otter moms do in the wild. "Tilly has been teaching Ziggy to do some deep dives. Otter pups are very buoyant, so it takes them a little bit to learn how to go underwater." Ziggy learned quickly. "He's a little motorboat," said Christie.

Mom Tilly was rescued as an injured orphan at only four months old and rehabilitated by keepers at the Oregon Zoo.

Cotton-top Tamarin CR
Zoo Basel, Switzerland

In cotton-top tamarin communities, the queen rules!
The dominant female is the only one allowed to
breed. Not only does she lay down the law socially,
but she also releases powerful pheromones that deter
younger females from breeding.

When the queen's one or two babies arrive, the
whole group cares for them, although the males tend
to do most of the work, including protecting, grooming, and playing with the youngsters. Researchers
have spent considerable time trying to understand
the evolutionary benefits to this seemingly altruistic
behavior among male cotton-tops.

Capybara  LC
Paignton Zoo, UK

It's hard to hide when you're the world's largest rodent! At four feet long or bigger, capybaras do their best to stay out of sight—or at least out of reach—by lounging in swamps and rivers. While they give birth to their litter of around four pups on land, the young join mom for a swim at just a few days old. If they feel particularly threatened, capybaras can dive underwater for up to five minutes before surfacing.

Capybara moms share parenting duties, including nursing one another's young. Moms nuzzle their young to calm them, clean them, and build bonds.

Snow Leopard EN

Zoo Basel, Switzerland

Mother snow leopard, Mayhan, ventured outside for the first time with her six-month-old cubs, who proved to be bold and curious. Perhaps because of the harsh conditions of their cold mountain homes, most snow leopard moms give birth around the same time of year, which is unusual among big cats.

Red Kangaroo LC

Keepers noticed a distinct change in Skippy's behavior after she gave birth to Ramiro, her first joey. While Skippy had previously been quite shy, once her joey started to peek his head out of her pouch, she would lounge in the front of the exhibit, seemingly showing off her new baby.

For a first-time mom, Skippy proved very attentive. If Ramiro strayed too far away, she would make chuffing noises to call him back.

A common marsupial misconception is that a kangaroo's pouch is simply a pocket. In reality, the opening of a kangaroo's pouch has strong muscles that a mother 'roo can contract to keep her joey securely in place while she bounces to her next stop.

Pot-bellied Pig

Tiergarten Delitzsch, Germany

For a pig, few things beat playing with mom in the mud! This pot-bellied pig mom's name is Fine, but for medical reasons she struggled to successfully birth piglets. Luckily this little piggy thrived. Mom and piglet bonded closely.

Pot-bellied pigs are a domestic breed that originated in Vietnam and have proven popular as pets. While smaller than most domestic pigs, many would-be owners don't realize this breed is likely to reach 125 lbs (57kg) or more in adulthood.

Tiergarten Delitzsch

Sumatran Tiger <small>CR</small>

Sacramento Zoo, California

At bath time, mother Sumatran tiger, Bahagia, hugs her cub
with her front legs and administers licks, both reinforcing
bonds and holding her rambunctious cub, CJ, still.

Critically endangered, only a few hundred Sumatran tigers
remain between conservation-focused zoos and the wild.

King Penguin
St. Louis Zoo, Missouri

King penguin parents share the responsibility of raising their young, and Saint Louis Zoo's penguin couple, Francine and Kaiju, were no exception. Chicks hatch after fifty-five days and this little one weighed just seven ounces (less than half a pound) at birth. Though small at birth, king penguins grow into the largest and most handsome adult penguins. At 33lbs (15kg), they are second only to the emperor penguin.

Ray Meibaum / Saint Louis Zoo

© Houston Zoo, Stephanie Adams

Nyala LC
Houston Zoo, Texas

At 3:55 PM mother nyala, Ginger, went into labor at the Houston Zoo. By 4:02 PM, less than seven minutes later, little Peanut was born, making for one of the fastest deliveries ever witnessed by Zoo staff. Over the next three months, Houston Zoo welcomed two more nyala calves, thrusting Peanut into the role of protective older brother.

In the wild, nyalas typically give birth in thick bushes to hide their vulnerable calves from predators.

Mike Owyang / Sacramento Zoo

Wolf's Guenon LC

Sacramento Zoo, California

Mama guenon, Mimi, was an outstanding first-time mother: always attentive and anticipating baby Zuri's needs before she made a fuss.

When Zuri was just old enough to leave mom for a few minutes but not old enough to explore on her own, Mimi would place Zuri in a planter that served as a playpen. With Zuri safely contained, Mimi could steal a few minutes of personal time. Zookeepers never imagined that the planter might be used in that way.

In the wild, this species lives in dense forests making them hard to observe. Research conducted at zoos like Sacramento has proven invaluable in under-standing the biology and behavior of this colorful and playful Old World monkey.

88

California Sea Lion LC

Pictured at just a few days old, this tiny pup was born to four-year-old mom, Marina. Mom came to Seneca Park Zoo from the Marine Mammal Care Center after being found stranded on a Los Angeles County beach.

Mother California sea lions nurse their pups for ten days then begin leaving for short periods of time to forage. During these periods, which can last up to a few days, the pups gather together in nurseries where they cuddle, rough house, and vocalize. When mom returns, mother and pup reunite by recognizing one another's unique bark and cry, respectively.

While father sea lions don't play an active role in parenting, they have been observed protecting pups from sharks and orcas.

Christopher Morabito / Seneca Park Zoo

Marissa Smithker / Sebeca Park Zoo

Giant Anteater

VU

Nashville Zoo, Tennessee

Anteater pups ride on mom's back for the first ten months of life. Mother and pup's black stripes line up with one another to preserve their camouflage.

Typically solitary animals, during courtship male and female anteaters will sometimes slurp ants from the same termite mound—the anteater version of sharing a milkshake!

© Amiee Stubbs

Tampa's Lowry Park Zoo

Siamang EN
Tampa's Lowry Park Zoo, Florida

A tiny, lanky baby siamang sprawls out on first-time mother Haddie's tummy at Tampa's Lowry Park Zoo. Siamang's are best known for their unique songs, and mated pairs will sing long, loud duets. Researchers believe these duets enable pairs to broadcast their close bond, warding off other siamangs who might otherwise venture into their territory. Siamang pairs are monogamous and both mom and dad raise their young.

Fort Worth Zoo

Jaguar NT
Fort Worth Zoo, Texas

Four-year-old jaguar mom, Xochi (zo-she), welcomed healthy 2 lb (.9 kg) cub, Sasha, in a private, off-exhibit area, as jaguars prefer to give birth in a secluded place. In the wild, jaguar cubs depend on their mothers for food, guidance, and protection from predators until about two years of age. Mother jaguars don't trust males around their cubs and will aggressively chase them off if they come too close.

The Fort Worth Zoo participates in the Association of Zoos and Aquariums (AZA) Jaguar Species Survival Plan (SSP), a breeding program that maintains a healthy, self-sustaining population of vulnerable animals to help prevent their extinction.

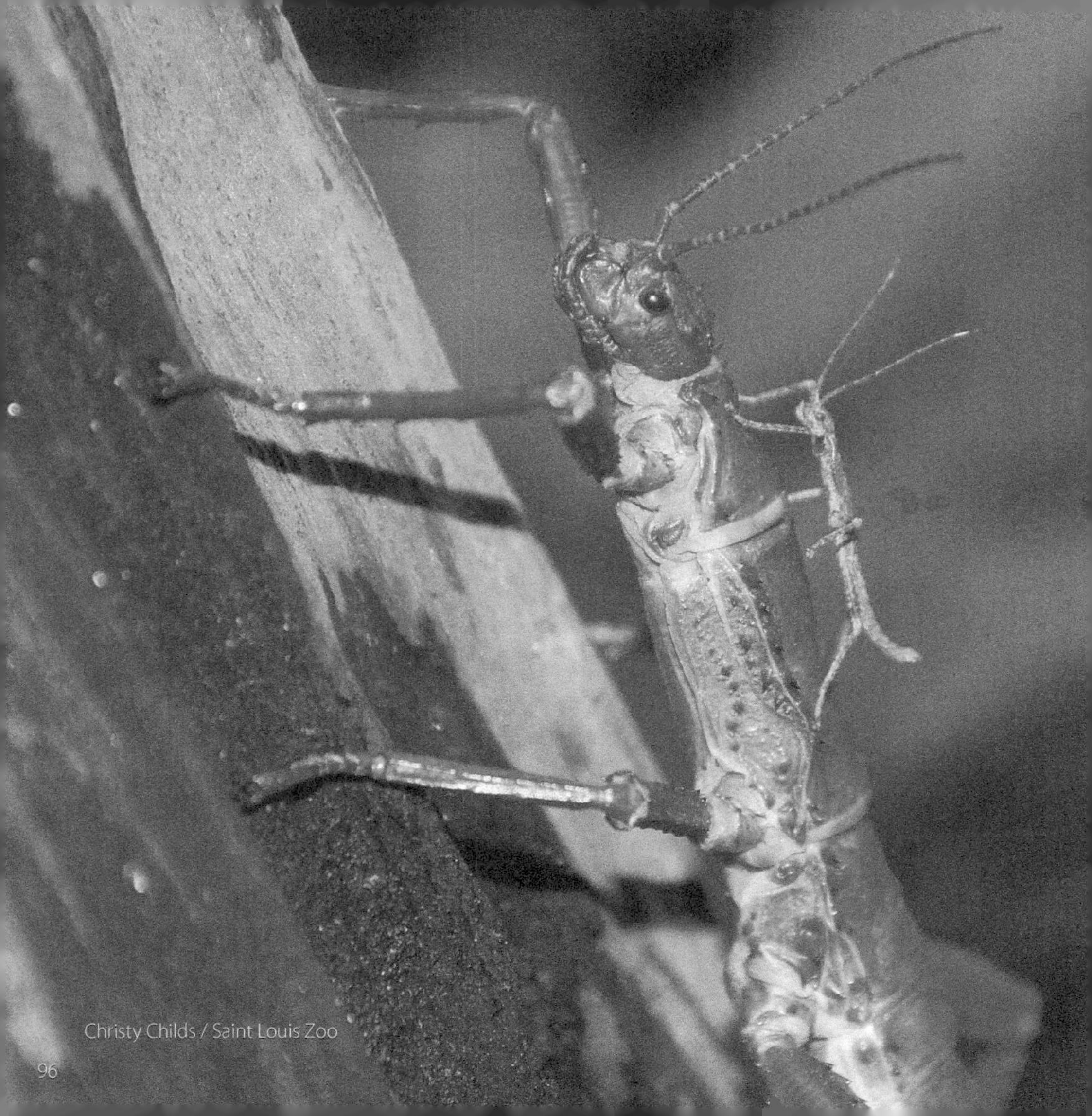

Christy Childs / Saint Louis Zoo

Giant Spiny Walkingstick LC

Giant spiny walkingsticks aren't the most nurturing parents, typically laying eggs and moving on. However, what they lack in parenting skills, they make up for in miraculous reproductive abilities.

When no males are available, female giant walkingsticks can exhibit parthenogenesis, the ability to reproduce without fertilization. Their hatchlings are clones; exact genetic copies of mom.

Giant spiny walkingsticks live up to their name, growing to half a foot (15 cm) in length.

African Spurred Tortoise

Linton Zoo, UK

Meet African spurred tortoise mom, Kali, whose name means "energetic" in the Senufo language spoken in Ivory Coast, Mali, and Burkina Faso. The name is fitting for a mom who laid about half the eggs that resulted in this bumper crop of forty-five baby tortoises at Linton Zoo in the UK.

Female tortoises dig out a depression two feet deep to lay their eggs. Since Britain's climate is quite different from this tortoise's native home in Sub-Saharan Africa, keepers collected the eggs and incubated them until hatching.

African spurred tortoises are the third largest in the world after the Galapagos and Aldabra tortoises, respectively. Since tortoise hatchlings are self-sufficient and adults are gigantic, reaching 200 lbs (90 kg), babies typically live behind the scenes for their safety, but keepers brought them together for this quick photo shoot.

Dwarf Mongoose LC
Edinburgh Zoo, UK

Dwarf mongoose parents Elvina and Elmo wasted no time in delighting Edinburgh Zoo with a trio of kits shortly after their arrival. They had their paws full with their bold offspring, who began exploring the tunnels in their enclosure within days of birth. In the wild, dwarf mongoose moms give birth underground in abandoned termite mounds, so it's no wonder the kits take naturally to subterranean adventure.

Playful, curious, and highly social, dwarf mongooses live in groups of up to twenty individuals and all members contribute in helping to raise the young. When the group goes foraging, typically a mongoose or two will remain behind to babysit.

Dwarf mongooses are the world's smallest mongooses and Africa's smallest carnivore.

Edinburgh Zoo

Belfast Zoological Gardens

Red Titi Monkey LC

Belfast Zoo, Ireland

Red titi monkeys are unusual among primates, as males and females mate for life. Mother, Inca, and father, Aztec, are Belfast Zoo's inseparable couple. They love to sit and sleep with their tails intertwined. With the arrival of this new baby, it was Aztec who had his hands full as male titi monkeys play the lead role in parenting, typically caring, carrying, and protecting the young. In fact, the more experienced the mom, the less time she spends with the baby!

For the first few weeks, newborns will hang from dad's neck but will eventually clamber onto dad's back and shoulders to ride piggyback.

Belfast Zoo has been home to red titi monkeys since 2010, when mom and dad arrived from the London Zoo and Blackpool Zoo, respectively.

Eurasian Moose  ⓛⓒ
Wildpark Potzberg, Germany

When momma moose, Sophie, had her first calf in 2007, she was inattentive and keepers stepped in to hand-raise her baby moose. So when Sophie became pregnant with her second calf, keepers were worried. Fortunately Sophie allayed their fears, lavishing her calf with attention and jealously guarding him from keepers and other moose alike.

Because Sophie was so protective, keepers had to guess at the calf's sex and pick a name before knowing for sure. They guessed wrong and so little Ellie is a male moose who makes do with a female name. Luckily, Ellie doesn't seem to mind.

After preventing other moose from greeting her new calf for the first two weeks, Sophie finally relented when Ellie decided to venture off and meet the herd. The introduction went very smoothly; it didn't hurt that Sophie is the alpha female of the group!

Wildpark Potzberg feed their herd fresh shrubs daily. The moose gobble up the leaves and chew off the bark. Even with an abundant supply and variety of branches, keepers must fence off the trees in the habitat or the moose will chew off all the bark.

Ramona Hasse

Spotted Hyena LC

Monarto Zoo, Australia

Hyena cub Pinduli was born without incident but just a few weeks later his older sister, Forest, underwent Australia's first hyena caesarean! Given their unique anatomy, first time hyena moms have only a 20% chance of a successful natural outcome. Veterinarians decided to intervene after it became clear Forest was struggling. Keepers knew all was well when Pinduli nipped a nurse at the start of his exam.

Southern White Rhinoceros ^{NT}

Monarto Zoo, Australia

Monarto Zoo's female white rhino, Umqali, is a fantastic mother who successfully raised three calves before her most recent arrival, Digger. Umqali was very protective of Digger and would rarely let keepers get close enough to examine her baby. Eventually, Digger learned that the keepers provide excellent back scratches and now he makes a point of saying hello.

Digger was born on an Australian military holiday called ANZAC Day (Australia New Zealand Army Corps) and the term "digger" is slang in Australia for military personnel.

Pregnancy for white rhinoceroses is a long process, often lasting eighteen months. Calves can weigh 140 lbs (63 kg) or more. While that may sound big for a baby, it's relatively small when compared to their average adult size of up to 4,000–5,000 lbs (1,800–2,250 kgs).

Red Panda ⓥⓤ

Lincoln Children's Zoo, Nebraska

Mother red panda, Sophia, gave birth at Scotland's Edinburgh Zoo to two feisty cubs, one of which grew up to become a world famous escape artist! One year later, Rusty was living at the Smithsonian National Zoo when heavy rains caused nearby tree limbs to sag, creating a perfect bridge for Rusty to climb out of his enclosure. His adventure through Washington D.C. was short-lived before he was returned but caused a media sensation.

Red pandas give birth to one to four cubs and shuffle them between nest boxes, presumably to elude would-be predators. After three months, the very curious and playful cubs begin to venture out and look for trouble.

Observing red pandas in the wild is challenging, so population estimates are uncertain, but the population trend appears to be decreasing. Organizations like the Red Panda Network work with local populations in China, Nepal, and India to protect this unique species.

Davi Ann / Lincoln Children's Zoo

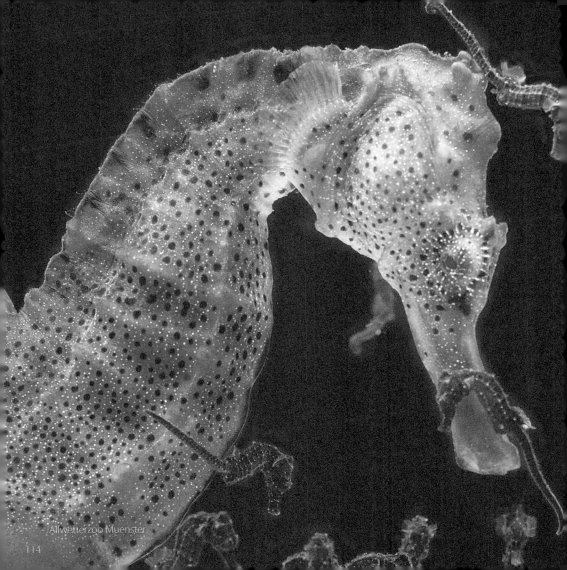

Allwetterzoo Muenster

Slender Seahorse ⓓⓓ

Allwetterzoo Münster, Germany

While males of many species help care for their young, male seahorses actually give birth. After fertilization, female seahorses deposit the eggs in the male's pouch where he nourishes them for weeks before they emerge. Pictured here, a father slender seahorse glides along with his two hundred newly birthed babies.

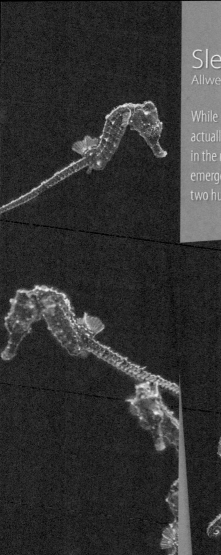

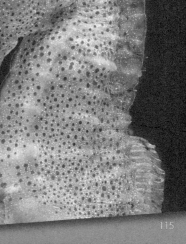

Grevy's Zebra  EN
Denver Zoo, Colorado

An experienced zebra mom, Topaz has raised three healthy foals. In this photo, she carefully shepherds her one-month old foal around the yard.

Mom stays close to ensure her foal recognizes her unique stripes and smells. When mother zebras head out to forage, they leave their young with other foals in a "kindergarten," which is typically guarded by a large male.

Topaz and the foal's father, Punda, were paired under recommendation of the Association of Zoos and Aquariums (AZA) Species Survival Plan (SSP), which ensures healthy populations and genetic diversity among zoo animals.

Denver Zoo

Two-toed Sloth

Lincoln Park Zoo, Chicago, Illinois

Pictured at just one week old, this tiny Hoffmann's two-toed sloth clings to mom's furry tummy at Chicago's Lincoln Park Zoo, where it remained for the first nine weeks of its life. Despite being a first-time mom and twenty years old, this sloth mother proved affectionate and attentive to her baby's needs.

Baby sloths are born with their claws developed, ensuring they can grab onto mom immediately after birth. This is essential since they are often born high in the trees with mom hanging from a branch!

John Kortas / Lincoln Park Zoo

Eastern Bongo  CR
Houston Zoo, Texas

Brody the baby bongo was born a robust 40 lbs (18.3 kg). Thanks to a healthy appetite, he more than doubled his weight in only five weeks, reaching 92 lbs (42 kg)! For the first few weeks of his life, he stayed close to his mom, Penelope, but in the wild they would see a lot less of each other. Wild bongo moms deposit their babies in secluded spots and return intermittently to feed their young.

To the casual observer, bongo calves may look alike but Houston Zoo keepers found a way to keep their multiple calves straight by counting the white stripes on their sides.

Critically endangered due to poaching and habitat destruction, Eastern bongos are bred and reintroduced into the wild as part of a Species Survival Plan.

Red Brocket DD
Gladys Porter Zoo, Brownsville, Texas

Native to dense tropical forests in Central and Southern America, little is known about this diminutive deer, which reaches only thirty inches tall at the shoulder in adulthood.

Pictured at just two weeks old, this fawn is one of only a handful of brocket deer to be born at US zoos, where the species is rarely exhibited.

Patricia Scanlan / Gladys Porter Zoo

Bornean Orangutan ⒠

Paignton Zoo, UK

Pictured at just a few days old, baby Tatau was born to mom, Mali. Their bond was obvious and immediate. While Tatau spent her first few months clinging to Mali, her fingers intertwined with mom's fur, at one year old she was beginning to develop her climbing skills. "She explores, but still does not venture far from mum," explained Paignton Zoo staff. "She is doing well. Her progress is fairly typical for a one-year old orang. She is not weaned yet, but tries any food that is passing on the way to mum's mouth! She picks at the watery, soft items like cucumbers and tomatoes, but is mainly just sucking on them wistfully!"

Orangutan moms typically don't give birth to their first baby until age fifteen and nurse their babies for four years or more. Much like humans, the path to adulthood is long and requires a tremendous amount of mothering. Also much like humans, young orangs will seek out other juveniles to play with.

Bornean orangutans are threatened by habitat destruction for palm oil production. Palm oil is found in many products and everyone can help these animals by reading labels at the grocery store and avoiding products that include this ingredient.

Ray Wiltshire / Paignton Zoo

121

Baird's Tapir
Nashville Zoo, Tennessee

Nashville Zoo Animal Care Staff waited more than 13 months for the arrival of this little Baird's Tapir. Soon after the calf's delivery it became clear that something was wrong. The baby's embryonic sac did not break, so the calf could not breathe. Zoo staff made the decision to intervene and moved mother Houston out of the stall. They freed the baby from the sac, immediately cleared his airways and performed mouth-to-snout resuscitation until he was fully breathing on his own. Thanks to these heroic efforts and quick action, the calf was saved.

Since named Felix, the miraculous baby became a social media star and continues to thrive.

Chilean Flamingo NT

Woodland Park Zoo, Seattle, Washington

Both male and female Chilean flamingo parents care for their chicks, feeding them "crop milk," which is nutritionally similar to milk that is produced by mammals. The chicks leave their nest about three to five days after hatching but remain in close proximity to their parents for feedings and brooding.

Flamingo chicks hatch with a whitish, gray down and acquire extensive pink feathering that can be mixed with gray-brown contour feathers at about one year of age. Juveniles usually have full pink feathering by two to three years of age.

Dennis Dow / Woodland Park Zoo

African Lion VU

Woodland Park Zoo, Seattle, Washington

Lioness Adia had her paws full with the arrival of four cubs, two girls, named Nobuhle and Busela, and two boys, named Pelo and Rudo. Woodland Park Zoo keepers did their best to keep the cubs busy by filling the yard with mossy logs, muddy pits, and sticks for the cubs to play with, but their favorite toy was always mom. They constantly pounced on her, grabbed her neck, or slipped under her feet. New distractions, like planes flying overhead and cawing birds also caught the cubs' attention and provided mom with an occasional break.

In the wild, mother lions typically keep their cubs separated from the pride for up to two months after birth. However, if another lioness has also given birth around the same time, a mother lion may return earlier and the two moms will nurse and protect one another's cubs.

Ryan Hawk / Woodland Park Zoo

Meerkat LC
Perth Zoo, Australia

Born in the safety of the nest box at Perth Zoo, this trio of meerkat kits began venturing out at just three weeks old to play and explore. The first emergence of kits from a burrow (or nest box, in this case) is a big event in a meerkat mob and the entire group eagerly greets the new arrivals.

Highly social animals, the entire mob pitches in to help rear the kits. Other females without kits will even nurse the young. When the group goes foraging, an adult or two will remain behind to protect the kits, rushing them into the burrow at any sign of danger and then defending them fiercely. If they are too far from the burrow and threatened, the adult will climb on top of the kits to shelter them.

Zoo Salzburg

132

South American Tapir ⓥⓤ
Zoo Salzburg, Austria

Tapir mom, Bibi, welcomed her first calf, a healthy, five-pound girl, and the two spent the first few weeks playing, cuddling, and napping in the seclusion of their behind-the-scenes room.

Despite their large size and unique snout, which is actually a short, prehensile trunk, the tapir has received relatively little conservation attention. In their native Brazil, "tapir" is common slang for "slow" or "stupid" and most citizens don't know much about the species, if they've heard of it at all.

The International Union for the Conservation of Nature lists the South American Tapir as vulnerable due to the 30% population decline that has occurred over the past three generations. They are threatened by deforestation, competition with grazing livestock, and hunting. As large foragers, they are especially sensitive to this kind of habitat disruption.

David Haring / Duke Lemur Center

134

Blue-eyed Black Lemur

Duke Lemur Center, Durham, North Carolina

At birth little Hiddleston weighed less than three ounces (82 g) but first-time mom, West, was very gentle with her newborn. Blue-eyed black lemurs are dichromatic, meaning males and females have different color fur, black and red, respectively, though both males and females have striking blue eyes. (Hiddleston is named after actor Tom Hiddleston, aka Loki in the Thor and Avenger movies, who has striking blue eyes, too.)

The Duke Lemur Center (DLC) currently houses North America's only breeding females of blue-eyed black lemurs: West, Margaret, and Foster. These females hold the key to the conservation of this species of lemur because of dramatic habitat loss in the wild and the limited breeding population in captivity. With expert care (and some very handsome blue-eyed black lemur males), DLC is hoping for many more babies in the future to continue to preserve these rare, beautiful lemurs.

Asian Elephant EN
Oregon Zoo, Portland, Oregon

Lily the elephant calf loves taking a dip and frolicking with mom, Rose-Tu, at the Oregon Zoo. Elephants are excellent swimmers and can use their trunks as snorkels to breathe underwater. When not swimming, Lily can be found running around her enclosure, living up to her reputation as a spirited, energetic youngster.

Oregon Zoo Director, Kim Smith, explained, "[Lily] is vocalizing loudly. The first time we heard her, the sound was so deep and loud that we thought it was one of the older elephants. She's definitely got a great set of pipes, and it looks like she's going to be a real pistol."

Spectacled Bear (VU)
Planckendael Zoo, Belgium

In these photos, a young cub named Oberon ventures out of his den for the very first time. While spectacled bears are great climbers, Oberon proved quite a daredevil, immediately scaling the enclosure's trees. Mom, Zamora, was patient and trusting, permitting her little rascal to explore at a frantic pace.

Jonas Verhulst / Planckendael

Bat-eared Fox LC
Zoo Praha, Czech Republic

Unlike any other dog or fox, male bat-eared foxes take primary responsibility for raising pups after birth, including feeding, protecting, grooming, and playing with the pups, often staying in the den while mom goes out to hunt.

This Fox Father of the Year candidate has raised thirty pups since his arrival at Prague Zoo in 2007!

Cape Porcupine

LC

Zoo Basel, Switzerland

Baby porcupines are born with soft quills that harden within the first few hours after birth. Quills are in fact specially modified hairs that are sheathed in keratin—the same substance that forms human fingernails. Like many rodents, Cape porcupines grow rapidly, reaching up to two feet from snout to tail in adulthood.

Zoo Basel's porcupines are clicker-trained, which allows zoo keepers to better monitor the health and well-being of these nocturnal animals, who would rather hide than interact with keepers. The porcupines have learned that a click means they'll receive a tasty snack so they eagerly emerge from their hiding places.

Zoo Basel

Sumatran Orangutan CR
Zoo Atlanta, Georgia

Little Pongo was born via caesarean section on the advisement of a team of veterinarians and human medical experts after mom's first pregnancy was unsuccessful. Until he was three months old, Pongo received 24-hour nursery care from Zoo Atlanta staff and nursery volunteers while efforts continued to reintroduce him to mom, Blaze. Their hard work and dedication paid off; Pongo and Blaze now live together full time and share a close bond.

Kirk's Dik-dik LC
Chester Zoo, UK

When little Aluna was rejected by her mom, Chester Zoo's Curator of Mammals Tim Rowland, stepped in to care for the tiny Kirk's dik-dik antelope. The regimen included five bottle feedings a day, so wherever Tim went, Aluna went.

Tim outlined the routine. "Our little one is growing stronger and stronger by the day and, all being well, it shouldn't be too long until she'll be able to really hold her own. For the time being though, her feed times are staggered through the day and she has her first bottle in my living room at home at around 7AM. I then pop her into the car and bring her to work where she has another three feeds in my office. Finally, her last one is at 10 PM back at my house."

Chester Zoo

Echidna LC
Taronga Zoo, Australia

Typically baby echidnas remain in the burrow for their first fifty days, but Beau, as he was named, walked out into the wide world at only forty days old. So for the next few weeks, Annabelle served as Beau's mom.

Echidnas do not nurse their young in the same way as other mammals. Instead, they drip milk out of specialized milk patches. Rather than give Beau a bottle, Annabelle let Beau slurp up milk from the palm of her hand. While feeding, Beau resembled a mini vacuum cleaner, going back and forth making sure every drop of milk was sucked up.

Eventually Beau grew quills like all adult echidnas, but at the time of this photograph he had only a rough covering of hair that nurses referred to as his "five o'clock shadow."

Ben Gibson / Taronga Conservation Society Australia

149

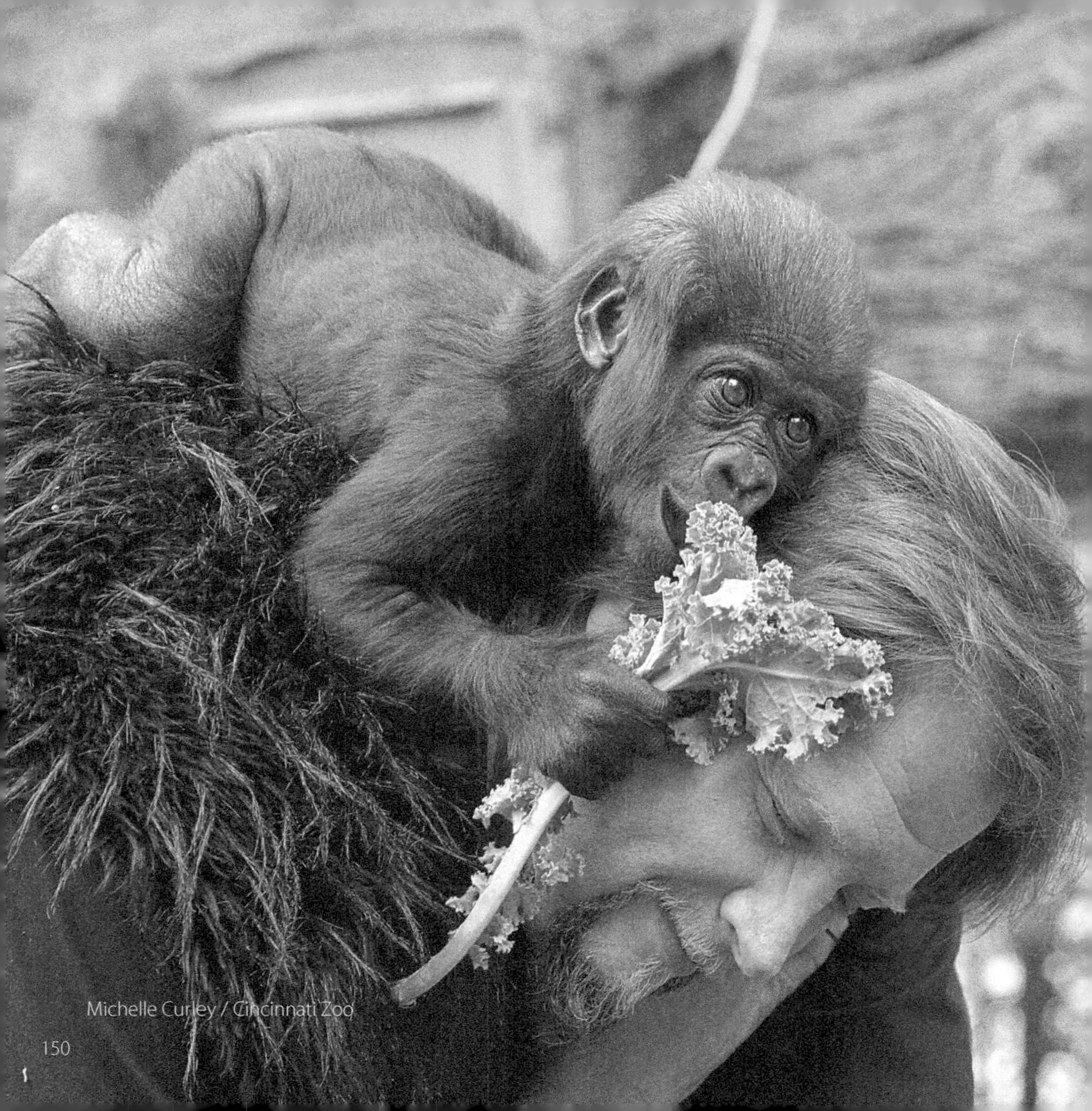
Michelle Curley / Cincinnati Zoo

Western Lowland Gorilla CR
Cincinnati Zoo & Botanical Garden, Ohio

Gorilla parenting doesn't always go according to plan—as was the case for little Gladys, whose birth mother was not as attentive as she could have been. Keepers working with Gladys wore a gorilla suit hoping to ease her eventual transition back with other gorillas. After a few weeks of round-the-clock human care, experts decided it would be best to relocate Gladys to the Cincinnati Zoo where she might find a potential surrogate mother.

Over the next few months, keepers slowly introduced Gladys to four adult females as part of their "gorillification process." Female M'Linzi quickly stepped up and became Gladys' surrogate mom. When troop leader, silverback Jomo, accepted Gladys shortly thereafter, the transition was complete! Today Gladys is a happy and healthy juvenile Western lowland gorilla.

INDEX BY ANIMAL

INDEX BY ZOO

Thanks to the institutions and individuals that made *ZooBorns* possible:

Aalborg Zoo
Adelaide Zoo
Akron Zoo
Al Ain Wildlife Park & Resort
Alaska SeaLife Center
Alma Park Zoo
Antwerp Zoo
Apenheul Primate Park
Aquarium of the Bay
Aquarium of the Pacific
Artis Zoo
Assiniboine Park Zoo
Auckland Zoo
Audubon Zoo
Australia Zoo
Aviarios Sloth Sanctuary
Banham Zoo
Belfast Zoo
Belgrade Zoo
Berlin Zoo
Besancon Zoo
Binder Park Zoo
Binghamton Zoo
Birch Aquarium
Blackpool Zoo
Bramble Park Zoo
Brevard Zoo
Bristol Zoo Gardens
British Wildlife Centre
Brookfield Zoo
Buffalo Zoo

Burgers Zoo
Busch Gardens
Calgary Zoo
California Academy of Sciences
Cango Wildlife Ranch
Cameron Park Zoo
Cape May County Zoo
Capron Park Zoo
Central Florida Zoo
Chattanooga Zoo
Chengdu Panda Base
Chessington Zoo
Chester Zoo
Chiang Mai Zoo
Chilean National Zoo
Cincinnati Zoo
Cleveland Metroparks Zoo
Colchester Zoo
Columbus Zoo & Aquarium
Como Zoo
Connecticut's Beardsley Zoo
Darmstadt Zoo
Denver Zoo
Detroit Zoo
Dierenrijk Europa Zoo
Diergaarde Blijdorp
Disney's Animal Kingdom
Dortmund Zoo
Dreamworld Australia
Dresden Zoo
Drusillas Park

Dublin Zoo
Dudley Zoo
Duke Lemur Center
Durrell Wildlife Conservation Trust
Dusit Zoo
Edinburgh Zoo
Edmonton Valley Zoo
Everland Zoo
Florida Aquarium
Fort Wayne Children's Zoo
Frankfurt Zoo
Georgia Aquarium
Great Plains Zoo
Hagenbeck Zoo
Hamilton Zoo
Hannover Zoo
Happy Hollow Zoo
Healesville Sanctuary
Hogle Zoo
Honolulu Zoo
Houston Zoo
Howlett's Wild Animal Park
Indianapolis Zoo
Jacksonville Zoo
Jardin des Plantes
Jerusalem Biblical Zoo
Johannesburg Zoo
Jurong Bird Park
Kangaroo Conservation Center
Kansas City Zoo
Knoxville Zoo

Kolmarden Zoo
Lakes Aquarium
Lee Richardson Zoo
Lincoln Children's Zoo
Lincoln Park Zoo
Linton Zoo
Lion Country Safari
Little Rock Zoo
Living Coasts Zoo
Longleat Safari Park
Loro Parque
Los Angeles Zoo
Louisville Zoo
Lowry Park Zoo
MacDuff Aquarium
Marwell Park Zoo
Maryland Zoo
Mata Ciliar Association
Melbourne Zoo
Memphis Zoo
Mesker Park Zoo
Mexicali Zoo
Milwaukee County Zoo
Minnesota Zoo
Mogo Zoo
Monkholm Zoo
Monterey Bay Aquarium
Moody Gardens
Mulhouse Zoo
Munster Zoo
Mystic Aquarium
M'Bopicuá Breeding Station
Naples Zoo

Nashville Zoo
National Aquarium in Baltimore
New England Aquarium
Newport Zoo
Newquay Zoo
Niabi Zoo
Norden's Ark
North Carolina Aquarium at Pine Knoll Shores
North Carolina Zoo
Northeastern Wisconsin Zoo
Oakland Zoo
Odense Zoo
Oklahoma City Zoo
Omahas Henry Doorly Zoo
Opel Zoo
Oregon Zoo
Osaka Aquarium Kaiyukan
Ouwehands Zoo
Paignton Zoo
Palm Beach Zoo
Park of Legends
Perth Zoo
Philadelphia Zoo
Phoenix Zoo
Pittsburgh Zoo
Planckendael Zoo
Point Defiance Zoo
Potter Park Zoo
Prague Zoo
Puerto Vallarta Zoo
Red River Zoo
Rio Grande Zoo

Riverbanks Zoo
Rome's Biopark Zoo
Rosamond Gifford Zoo
Rotterdam Zoo
Sacramento Zoo
Safari West
Saint Louis Zoo
Salisbury Zoo
San Diego Zoo
San Francisco Zoo
Santa Barbara Zoo
Scandinavian Wildlife Park
Schoenbrunn Zoo
Schwerin Zoo
Secret World Wildlife Rescue Center
Shedd Aquarium
Singapore Zoo
Smithsonian National Zoo
Southwick's Zoo
St. Augustine Alligator Farm Zoological Park
Stockholm Zoo
Sunshine International Aquarium
Taipei Zoo
Tallinn Zoo
Tama Zoo
Taronga Zoo
Tel Aviv Zoological Center
Tennessee Aquarium
The Fund for Animals Wildlife Center
Toledo Zoo
Toronto Zoo
Trotter's World

Tulsa Zoo
Twycross Zoo
Ueno Zoo
Virginia Living Museum
Virginia Zoo
WCS's Bronx Zoo
WCS's New York Aquarium
WCS's Prospect Park Zoo

WCS's Queens Zoo
Wellington Zoo
Wildlife Heritage Foundation
Wildlife World Zoo
Wilhelma Zoo
Wingham Wildlife Park
Woodland Park Zoo
Wuppertal Zoo

Zoo Atlanta
Zoo Basel
Zoo Duisberg
Zoo Miami
Zoo New England
ZooAmerica
ZSL London Zoo
ZSL Whipsnade Zoo

ABOUT THE AUTHORS

Andrew Bleiman is a lifelong animal nerd who graduated from the University of Pennsylvania with a degree in English literature and a yet-to-be-recognized minor in Baby Animalogy. He attributes his fascination with zoology and conservation to monthly childhood trips to the Wildlife Conservation Society's Bronx Zoo. He lives in Seattle with his wife, Lillian, and daughter, Avery.

Chris Eastland is a classically trained artist and freelance designer who studied and taught at the Charles H. Cecil Studios in Florence, Italy. Chris was formerly the Photography Editor for *Quest Magazine.* He now lives in Brooklyn, New York , with his wife, Jeannine, their son, Fletch, their cat, Georgie, and fish, Peppa and George.

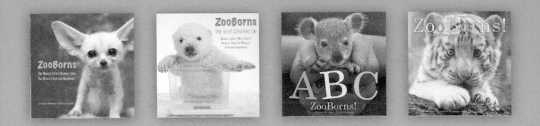

Don't miss all the other ZooBorns books, available wherever books are sold or at:

www.simonandschuster.com

And visit ZooBorns.com for the latest newborn arrivals!

www.zooborns.com